THE SILENCE:
WHAT IT IS AND HOW TO USE IT

by

DAVID V. BUSH

Author of "The Fundamentals of Applied Psychology", "Applied Psychology and Scientific Living", "Practical Psychology and Sex Life", "The Universality of the Master Mind", "Will Power and Success"

Editor, "Mind Power Plus"

Contents

Approach to the Silence

Wrong thinking produces inharmony in our body, which in turn produces sickness. Our bodies sometimes are instantly reharmonized while in the Silence. In the Silence our minds become passive, open, free and loving, at which time the Infinite Master of harmony touches the mental chords of our being and we are well.

Just as the piano can be tuned, so can the mind. Man's body is made up of twelve octaves the same as in music. All matter is music. All matter is composed of twelve octaves. Wrong thinking brings inharmony in some of the octaves of our body. Right thinking tunes these organs, puts them back into their normal condition.

Boys have their little steel magnets by which they pick up small pieces of steel, pins and so forth. When overworked, these magnets no longer attract. Then the boys take their magnets, have them rubbed against strong magnets or remagnetized with an electric current and their power is quickly restored—so with our bodies. Mind is the re-electrifier and re-harmonizer of the octaves into all harmony.

Right thinking, therefore, is the most important thing in life. As a man thinketh in his heart so is he. Just as a tuning fork near a piano will respond with a vibration when a key of the same pitch is struck on the piano nearby, so likewise do the bodies of men respond to proper stimulus and become in tune. By right thinking man can re-harmonize himself, can achieve health, success and prosperity.

To enter the Silence one must first establish perfect relaxation in mind and body. Then as the consciousness is brought from one part of the body to another the tuning takes place.

If the leader in the Silence should be intoning, there will be many in the audience who will feel tinkling sensations—vibrations—and often are instantly healed. They have been instantly re-harmonized. Sometimes it may take several intonings in the Silence for a complete healing. Should you have a violent vibration, feel no fear, but thank God for your healing because the more violent the vibration perhaps the worse has been your condition and the more surely has the re-harmony begun. Some people will feel this vibration for hours, even days, throughout which there is always healing.

Others may not feel the vibration at all, yet if there has been any inharmony in the bodily organs, these organs are unconscious to the conscious intoning re-harmonization. Many people who have been healed of divers and many malignant diseases were at no time conscious of any vibration. Never be discouraged if you feel no sensation. If you do feel a vibration, know that you are susceptible and on the high road to a healing demonstration.

The one intoning may or may not be feeling vibrations. Religion is the life of God in the soul of Man. The Silence is the medium by which the life of God and the soul of man are brought into At-one-ment.

The Silence is a medium by which man comes in a closer touch with the Infinite; a medium by which man becomes conscious of his nearness to the Infinite. The Silence is the meeting place where man's spirit links with God's spirit; where spirit meets spirit and the marvel of His grace never ceases.

The Silence is another way of praying, which is another way of concentration. It is another way of visualization.

"As a man thinketh in his heart so is he." In the Silence a man can by his thoughts change his life, his conditions, his environment, his all. By right thinking man becomes harmonious. A harmonious man—in tune with the Infinite—is on the King's highway to health, success, abundance, prosperity, happiness, love and peace.

By means of wrong thinking our minds are put out of harmony with the great Infinite spirit of God. "As a man thinketh in his heart so is he." When wrong thinking becomes right thinking, then man's right relationship to God is restored. He becomes an open channel for the influx of the spirit so that whatever demonstration he may desire he may have.

In the Silence a man may change his thinking as in no other way, therefore, may change his heart, change his whole being, change his environment, change every condition to which he was subject.

The human body may be likened to a harp. When man thinks rightly his body is in tune; but wrong thinking creates inharmony in the body and produces sickness. Wrong thinking produces inharmony in the mind, which, of course, disconnects man from rightful association with the Divine. A man must, therefore, think right. Yet, because of centuries of erroneous conception of God and of the world, man has been a negative instead of a positive being, and his unwisdom has reacted upon the present generation.

We are mental sending and receiving stations. What we receive depends upon how we are thinking Now. For success, health and happiness we must in the silent chambers of the soul change our thinking if we are holding negative or inharmonious thoughts. In the Silence there is presented to man his greatest opportunity to change his thinking. Wrong thinking produces inharmony of the body which in turn produces sickness. If we change to right thinking we have health, success and happiness. Therefore the Silence when properly used re-harmonizes our bodies and minds through the simple agency of right thinking.

"There are steps of approach to the Silence. Stillness is one thing and the Silence is another. One may quiet himself physically and not be still, and he may be still without entering the Silence. When one becomes physically and mentally at rest, he is apt to become receptive to psychic influences; and when these are not desired it is advisable to protect oneself while mentally negative. One may affirm his Oneness with God, his being surrounded and protected by the divine Goodness, and may symbolize this by enveloping himself in thought with the white light of love or the mellowed tints of sunshine.

"With the senses calmed and unresponsive to the slower vibrations, but responsive to the quicker ones, a peace and calm pervade one's mind, and it becomes consciously receptive to higher vibrations of vital energy. Immune from the lesser harmonies, one opens himself to the greater ones, which are always seeking avenues of expression. With the greater influx of the One Life, a sense of power steals over one and he becomes conscious of increased vigor and vitality.

"In relinquishing specific thoughts, one opens inwardly rather than outwardly, and becomes receptive to subconscious impressions that are directed by his conscious affirmation of fundamental Truth. The subconscious responds by returning to the conscious the logical sequences of the Truths that have been consciously impressed upon it. The subconscious follows the lead given to it by the conscious affirmations of Truth, and it brings back the consciousness of those Truths in their various ramifications."

Health Silence

Select one or more of the affirmations or formulas below to hold in thought while in the Silence. You may change or vary these as you choose:

> Soul is health, spirit is health, God is health, I am health. Since there is but one mind, there is but one mentality. This mind and mentality is God; God is health. I am health.
>
> "I am whole, perfect, strong, powerful, loving, harmonious and happy and what I am myself I desire for everyone else."
>
> "I am filled with the abundant, intelligent, ever-present life of Spirit. It flows through me freely, cleansing, healing, purifying and vitalizing every part. I am one with this life and in it I am every whit whole."
>
> "The all-powerful Christ Mind in me dissolves and dissipates every adverse thought. My body is the pure and Holy Temple of the Living God, and every organ and every function is now in Divine Order and Harmony."
>
> All the organs of my body are functioning normally and I amwell, whole and complete.

All is mind, all is God, all is universal energy. I am part of creative force and I am health, abundance, joy and peace.

I am filled, I am thrilled with Life Eternal and I radiate that life within to me and without to all.

Every experience of my life has been for my good and I am happy in living.

God is Spirit. I (use your own name) am life. Life Spirit is now flowing through me freely and I am well, whole and complete.

"Be still and know that I am God."

USE THE FOLLOWING AS A BASIS FOR YOUR MEDITATION AS YOU DEMONSTRATE HEALTH. OF COURSE, YOU MAY USE OTHER THOUGHTS PROVIDED THEY ARE CONSTRUCTIVE HEALTH THOUGHTS.

You may practice the Silence sitting, reclining, or in bed.

There is no better way to learn how to relax than by going into theSilence. Are you tense? Let go. Relax.

Then direct the mind to go from one part of the body to another. Take a deep breath between each change of your consciousness. Be sure to use the diaphragmatic or abdominal breathing—breathing through the nostrils, mouth closed until the muscles of the abdomen expand.

The best time to hold the Silence is as you retire at night, and just as you awaken in the morning.[2] But you should hold your thought at least three times a day, without stress or strain, without doubt or worry, passive in mind and body—perfectly relaxed.

Hold the Silence or thought upon retiring at night, awakening in the morning, and at noon day. Of course, you may take any other time that is convenient. You may concentrate on the roadway, street car, home or office, but it is well, if possible, to have one room for your Silence. Most people in that way will build up stronger vibrations. At noon now there are all over the world thousands of others holding Silence so that there is a great combined mental force working together at one time for success, health, prosperity and happiness, and we therefore get the benefit of this great vibration.

The more often you hold the Silence without stress or strain, as a rule, the quicker may be the demonstration.

The real part of me is Spirit, not matter. I believe that this body of mine is a Tabernacle for the Spirit. The real "I am" within me is therefore Spirit. The real "me" is Spirit.

This Spirit is the God Spirit. This is what Jesus meant when in the fourteenth chapter of John and again in the seventeenth chapter of the same Gospel, speaking to His Disciples He referred to "I in you, you in Me and We in God."

My Spirit is a part of the God Spirit. God is health, God is perfection, God is abundance, God is harmonious. Therefore, the real "I am" is God; the real "I am" is health, perfection, abundance and harmony.

When I am sick I know that it is the material of me that is sick, not the God Spirit; it is my *physical* being which is out of harmony, it is this Tabernacle of which Paul speaks, housing my spirit, which gives me pain and suffering. The real "me" is not sick, it is *my body*.

For centuries we have held to a wrong idea of life. We have thought that life is material; but life is spiritual, it is the invisible within me which is eternal, which is God. Many still believe that life is material and matter, instead of mind and spirit. I no longer hold that conception. I believe that all is mind and Spirit.

Just here is where the healing methods of drugs and the scientist's explanation of life is so limited. Not until we recognize that life is really a thing of spirit—not matter but mind—not material but spiritual—do we come into an understanding of Truth.

Jesus said, "God is Spirit," and on different occasions told His Disciples that this Spirit was within them as well as within Himself. Therefore, this same Spirit is within me and this same Spirit is the God Spirit of health, abundance, happiness, harmony and perfection.

God is all health, all abundance, all harmony, peace and perfection. Therefore the God Spirit within me is the same. I am sick in body; not in mind, not in Spirit.

Inasmuch as I cannot conceive of God being sick neither can I conceive of my Spirit being sick. My spirit is health, perfection and harmony. My body may not be well, but since mind is all, since this material is subject to the spiritual, since matter is subject to mind, I believe and affirm that my health does not depend upon matter but upon the God Spirit within me. It depends not upon the material but the spiritual, upon the God mind within.

Just as wood when made into a violin and properly tuned, will give forth harmony, so my body, though made in the material, when properly tuned by mind will give forth harmonious living, perfect health.

As the tree standing in the forest may be made into the violin music box of harmony, so my body, the material in the forest of matter, may be put in tune, become harmonious and be raised to perfection by the Master Musician, God—His mind within me.

God is all health. No one could conceive of God as being sick. I can visualize only the eternal spirit of the Infinite Father. Perfection existing in everything and I being a child in Spirit, am well, whole and complete in Spirit. My real "I am" is well.

Science now asserts that matter is composed of twelve octaves, just as in music. My body is the composite of these twelve octaves. Science also says that every cell atom, every electron in my body is intelligent.

This spirit of mine is housed in the Tabernacle of the body which is composed of millions and millions of cells, all of which having intelligence respond in my body according to the way I think. Every word I entertain, every thought I hold, influences everyone of the millions of cells making up this Tabernacle.

My body is made whole and complete physically. That is, all the cells of my body are made over new every eleven months. The body I have today is not the body I had eleven months ago. I get a new body every eleven months and my body is today what my thinking was yesterday, the day before that and the months before that. My body in the future depends upon my thinking in the future. I am what I think I am.

When I affirm that I am well, whole and complete; that I am perfect, harmonious and strong, I am suggesting to every atom in my body perfection and every atom in turn begins to make my body over, new in health and and in perfection.

I may or I may not have to wait for the element of time to make over every cell. That may be done spontaneously and instantly. There is no limitation to the power of God so I shall not set a time limit for my healing, knowing that all things are possible with the Father. I affirm that now I have that which I desire. I know that now the Spirit of divine health is surging through me, touching and reaching every atom of my body and that now the God Spirit within me is perfect and that Spirit makes my body perfect.

"Man is a Spiritual Being. Man expresses himself mentally and manifests himself physically. The One Life animates all that exists. Harmony of existence depends upon the polarities of the three aspects of life. The mind is at ease when open to the inflow of the Spirit. It is discordant when it follows sensory impressions. The body is healthy when responsive to the direction of the spiritualized mind. It becomes diseased when it accepts the physical as its guide. One achieves mental ease and physical health through his mental polarity. If open to the physical and closed to the spiritual, discord will prevail. If open to the spiritual and closed to the physical, he lives the One Life, in mental ease and physical health. I open my mind to the inflow of the Spirit. I place my body under the control of my spiritualized mind. I feel the One Life animate my mind and my body. I AM a Spiritual Being. I AM Perfect Health!"

Miscellaneous Silence[3]

THOUGHT TO HOLD IN THE SILENCE FOR ABUNDANCE

"The Universal Abundant Spirit Supplies All My Needs."

There is no want or limitation in the law. If, perchance, there should appear to be lack of, or need of, abundance in our lives, it is because of wrong thinking—not because there is a lack of abundance. Therefore, we should enter the Silence with the profound faith and conviction that the world is filled with plenty, and that all our needs are most bountifully supplied.

The mind should be saturated with the conviction that all life is filled with abundance—all space is overflowing with abundance—all living comes from an abundant source of supply.

In a Universe where this is true, there can be no want, no lack for you or yours (for me or mine).

As you take your exercises this month, take the affirmation above. As you walk on the street to your office, or place of business, continue this thought. As you go about your daily duties in the home or workshop, let the mind be saturated with a spirit, a feeling and thinking of abundance—"The opulence of the Universal Source of Supply now meets all my needs," "The Abundant Life Giving Spirit of Prosperity now leads and guides me into the paths of plenty, peace and power," "My mind is filled with prosperous thoughts, my being is pulsating in abundant rhythm, my soul is uplifted and sustained by a thousand thoughts of ever-present abundance, prosperity and opulence."

As these thoughts are maintained and repeated again and again, absorbed and sunk deep into the subconscious mind, know that all of your needs are this minute supplied. Know that you could not ask for anything from the Universal Spirit—Father, God—without that Spirit being most willing to supply, instantly, all your needs. The spirit and body are well, but the flesh is weak. Allow your flesh to be stimulated, and your body to respond by thoughts of abundance, prosperity and opulence.

"I am now rich in thought, rich in body and rich in spirit. I am now part of the abundant ever-present spirit of prosperity and opulence. All that I need is now mine, mine, mine."

The Universal Abundant Spirit supplies all my needs.

Thought to Hold in Meditation in the Silence

FOR MISFORTUNES, GRIEF, MISTAKES, REVERSES, FAILURE, SORROW, LOSS AND DISAPPOINTMENT

"All is Good."

We are entering upon a new consciousness for the human race, a higher plane of mentality, and a greater development of the spiritual life.

In spirit, of course, there is no wrong, no sorrow, no grief, no misfortune, no losses, no reverses. In short all is perfection.

The age in which we are living has not yet developed this spiritual understanding. We are still of the earth—earthly—and we are still in that consciousness where the physical is affected by seeming misfortunes, reverses, sorrows, griefs, trouble, sickness, etc. We may be wise in not expecting that suddenly this generation of man will reach that spiritual plane where there will be no recognition of anything except good.

We are a part of the Infinite Spirit ourselves and, of course, in spirit, we are perfection. But this physical body of ours manifests imperfection from time to time, because of our past training and past thinking, because of our own consciousness. In time there is no doubt in my mind but that the spirit within will make a perfect body without. This perfection will be recognized in health and in peace of mind. It will be recognized so that there will be no such thing as misfortunes, sorrows, reverses, failures, griefs, disappointments or losses being able to affect our mentality or our body. In this state of consciousness, as we are emerging from the chrysalis, material stage of man into the greater life, into the deeper spiritual understanding, we are subject to certain conditions not conducive to peace of mind without an effort. In other words, we recognize, or feel the effects of losses, misfortunes, disappointments, sorrows, griefs, etc. We recognize now, that the time is coming when the spirit will be so completely in control of matter in the body, that we will not recognize any inharmony. To reach that Great Spirit is one of the big forward steps in this generation. To reach that spiritual plane also means the right kind of thinking now. We plan, today, for tomorrow. This is true in every walk of life.

We plan our home today—and build it tomorrow. We make our merchandise today and market it tomorrow. We sow our seed today and we reap the harvest tomorrow. We build our career today, little by little, and we reach the outcome tomorrow. Therefore, our thinking today will change our tomorrow. The thinking of this generation will change the condition of tomorrow's generation. If tomorrow's generation is going to be free from the recognition of sorrows, misfortunes, griefs, fears, pain, losses, failures, reverses, inharmony, discord, etc., it depends upon our seed sowing.

Our seed sowing today should be "All is Good." All is Good in spirit. You can say that and be honest with yourself. All is perfection in spirit. All is good for us in spirit. All is good for our lives here. Spirit transcends matter. When we recognize, affirm, and continue to hold the constructive thought that All is Good in spirit, we are changing our own mental attitude, our own bodies, all matter in general—getting ready for the greater realization of the spiritual manifestation in the next generation.

Therefore, for your own good here today in success, prosperity and happiness as well as in health, peace and harmony, begin to pronounce over everything in life, *All is Good.* If you have any misunderstandings, *All is Good.* If you have any losses, *All is Good*, any reverses, *All is Good*, any sorrow, *All is Good*, any inharmony, *All is Good.* In everything at all that is out of perfection you must recognize only the good. ALL IS GOOD.

Sending your thought energy by repeating *All is Good*, and thinking *All is Good*, and living *All is Good*, you will actually, in this day, overcome your difficulty, and turn all of your mistakes, blunders and misfortunes into stepping stones for your own success, health and happiness.

I enter the Silence this month, this day, this hour and this minute. My mind is obsessed and under control of the Divine Spirit, I recognize here and now only good. I see in my fellowmen only perfection and good. I see in nature all around me only perfection and good. I see in every transaction of life only the perfect good. I see in every activity of my experience, and in every form, color and thought, good. *All is Good* for me now, today and forever.

God is spirit; spirit is love; love is perfection; God's spirit is harmonious, I am perfect, I am love, perfection and harmonious.

ALL IS GOOD.

For Harmony, Peace, Comfort

Base your thought for this Silence upon the following. You may add any constructive thought you choose.

"My Subconscious Mind, I Desire and Command You to Have Peace, Harmony and Justice Reign in the Hearts of Men Everywhere."

I realize that there can be no negative thinking for my destruction, downfall or harm sent out by anyone else that can reach my consciousness, or do me ill, unless I am afraid that such negative thinking will produce the evil effects others are planning.

I know that Thought is Energy. This is scientifically demonstrated, and I realize that a constructive thought has much more energy than a destructive thought. I know, because it has been conclusively proven, that constructive thinking will blast away every negative thought-current sent out by one person, or by a thousand.

Therefore, if there should be any inharmonious thoughts anywhere in the world—any discordant thought-current by those who seek my downfall, or block my progress, or by those who would endeavor to hurt my reputation—I know that by holding a harmonious attitude of peace, love, joy and success for everyone, including those who would do me wrong that such constructive thought-currents will blast away all of the discordant and inharmonious mental currents of evil so that they will not even reach my conscious mind.

I also realize, when I hold my silent thought, "*my subconscious mind I desire and command you to have peace and harmony and justice reign,*" that I am sending out the energy of construction which is bound to turn all of the efforts for my embarrassment and destruction into a higher current for my greater achievement.

Therefore, I send out blessings and thanksgiving to the very ones who would work my downfall. I charge my subconscious mind to let peace, harmony and justice reign so that all things will work together for the good for me and for those who are thinking evil.

If I should think it hard to send out blessings to my enemies, I remember the affirmation of the Greatest Teacher of all ages Who said, "Forgive until seventy times seven." I remember that when He, Himself, was reviled, reviled not in turn. I remember that when His merciless enemies had nailed Him to the cross, had apparently crushed His fondest ambition, had scorned and reviled the Kingdom of which He had spoken, and had tortured Him as He hung on the cross, He uttered the immortal, lovable, constructive words which have rung throughout the centuries, and will continue to bless all mankind throughout eternity: "Father, forgive them, for they know not what they do."

So those who would try to block my way, curb my progress or put thorns in my crown are doing so "not knowing what they are doing." "Whatsoever a man soweth, that shall he also reap." Instead of hurting me, they are sowing weed seeds, which shall bring forth a harvest of weeds and tares in their own lives, and not in mine.

I, therefore, do not wish them harm, nor think that they should feel the reaction. I do not have to concern myself about the negative people in the world—for the law takes care of them.

I shall always think constructive thoughts, harmonious thoughts and loving thoughts. "My Subconscious Mind, I desire and command you to have peace, harmony and justice reign, and know that all things are now working together for the good of my would-be enemies and for myself."

I relax (here pause and wait), take time for meditation (here pause and rest relaxed) and I become happy in the silence—holding my thought of peace, harmony and justice reigning in the hearts of men everywhere—and, as I relax and wait, I feel my vibrations rise. I am resting at ease, in faith. (Pause.) I am perfectly calm and contented. (Pause.) I am sending out love, peace and harmonious thoughts, and, as they go, love, peace and harmony will come to me. These are now returning. They enter my being and uplift my soul.

I am, therefore, sending out a strong current of spiritual blessings, with such a spirit of helpfulness, that I am getting back the same which I send out. My harvest shall be peace, love, joy, harmony, justice and contentment, because I am *sowing* the seed of love, peace, harmony, joy, contentment and justice into the great subconscious soil of the universe.

"My Subconscious Mind, I desire and command you to have peace, harmony and justice reign everywhere throughout the world."

I wait—I rest—I am relaxed—I am at ease and filled with the spirit of harmony. I wait. I listen for the spirit within. I feel and hear the voice of infinite love sending back into my consciousness these thoughts which I send out.

I know that my every constructive thought blasts away a thousand destructive ones. Therefore, I think peace, joy, love, harmony and justice, and, as I utter these words slowly and prayerfully, I feel my vibration rising—I experience ease of mind and peace of soul. Harmony is now within and without.

I realize that I cannot send out my affirmation of peace, love, joy and harmony without peace, love, joy and harmony coming back to me. I, therefore, send out my affirmation: "My Subconscious Mind, I desire and command you to have peace, harmony and justice reign-in the hearts of men wherever they may be." I wait and listen—perfectly relaxed and at ease—and I feel the vibrations which I sent out coming back to me.

I, therefore, know that no harm can befall my dwelling place. I know that whatever evil thoughts have been sent out for my destruction have been counter-blasted, and that now everything is working for my good.

As I recognize, and realize, that all things work together for my good, I am sending out love-thoughts that all things are working together for the good of those who would do me wrong. "They know not what they do." They alone will have to reap the harvest of the weeds they are sowing. My wish for them is that they may learn their lesson easily and early. My blessings I send out to them.

Again I wait. Again I listen. Again I am at ease, happy, and at rest. Love and blessings, peace and harmony, I send out—love and blessings, peace and harmony, come back. "My Subconscious Mind, I desire and command you to have peace, harmony and justice reign. My blessings upon all mankind—my love to everyone!"

Thought to Hold as a Basis for This Silence

FOR SUCCESS

"I Have Faith and Conviction in My Ultimate Success."

I believe the Scripture: "My ways are not your ways, saith the Lord; neither are my thoughts your thoughts, for as the heavens are higher than the earth, so are my thoughts higher than your thoughts."

I understand by this Scripture that the thoughts of the Infinite God are far above the understanding of finite me; that God's ways are higher than my ways. "God moves in a mysterious way His wonders to perform."

I also have faith and conviction in my ultimate success because I am a part of the Infinite Spirit, and in the Infinite Spirit, there can be no failure. I am harmonious, complete and successful in Spirit—in God.

I may not see my success today, or I may feel as though I have accomplished little, but I know that all my efforts and energies, in the past, present and future, are working together for my good.

Therefore, I shall hold the thought that my success has already been achieved. I am Success, I have success now and forever! Therefore, I think only success; I talk only success; I believe only in success; I am demonstrating success, and I know that success is mine.

The needed lessons I am having now, have had in the past, and may require in the future, are but necessary stepping stones to my greater success. The apparent delay of my greater success means that I am now demonstrating more success than I could otherwise have. Dreams that I have dreamed, visions that I have visualized, and the goal that I have mapped out, are all a part of my ultimate greater success. I have that now! I am successful now!

As Moses went into the land of Midian, and spent forty years of his life as a shepherd in the wilderness—(apparently with no future before him—which, however, was the great schooling necessary for his greater triumphant success in the future)—so I may be, in *my* land of Midian, apparently, only a sheep herder, but in reality getting the necessary training for my greater and ultimate success.

Therefore, I now rejoice in every experience I have—giving thanks for every apparent set back, and for every "seeming" blocking of my purposes and aspirations.

I believe that my past experiences, as well as present happenings, are for my benefit, and that I could not have been the great success I am, and shall be, had not the discouragements of yesterday, the perplexities of today and the drawbacks of tomorrow come into my life. I realize that I need to go into the land of Midian; that it is as necessary for me, as it was for Moses, to spend a few years in the wilderness of Life's experience. I am happy to know that I am in such company as that of the Great Leader of his people, and rejoice in the thought that the Lord has called me to spend my time in the land of Midian, getting the necessary training for the greater things the Lord has in store for me.

There is no place in the world where clouds do not gather, and storms do not rage; but when the storms abate, and the skies clear, then do we appreciate more fully the glories and beauties of God, the Universe and its natural laws, and Infinite Love.

However, I know by experience in the land of Midian, where clouds hover low, and where storms try the soul and body, that the dawn of a new day shall make life all the sweeter for me and mine.

Moses could not have enjoyed leading his people into the promised land, had he not been in the land of Midian. If he had stayed forever in the Court of Pharaoh, with its attendant luxuries, life would have taken on a dull, monotonous hue, and his experience would have seemed drab, wearisome and pale.

I am glad for the privilege accorded me to be in the land of Midian for a short time! I know that, as did Moses, I shall enjoy my promised land all the more when my greater success shall have been well worked out by the hand of Divinity.

Faith and conviction in my ultimate greater success is stronger today than ever! I hold such a strong thought, and such a deep and courageous faith in the workings of God's plan, that I know I now have that which has been intended for me, and nothing can take from me that which the Lord hath prepared for my success, health and happiness. I know, too, that I shall learn daily to enjoy, appreciate, and make better use of the success I now possess; that I shall unfold day by day into greater opportunities for more influence, power, friendship, charity, love, comradeship and service. I know that my present success is but a part of the greater success which the Lord has waiting for me—"just around the corner".

Therefore, I shall offer up prayers of thanksgiving and gratitude; I shall work harder, being more particular in the preparation for my greater work, than I have been in the past—never doubting but that every moment spent in this greater preparation will bring added interests, and a greater success in the future.

Even as Moses did not doubt the wisdom of the Lord for a greater future (when in the land of Midian for forty years), so shall I not doubt His ways today.

I claim, with a joyful heart and an attitude of thanksgiving, that my life could not have been as great in the future had I been denied my present experience. I know that greater things are in store for me, because God's thoughts are greater than my thoughts; because He is giving me that training now, in my land of Midian, which I most need. I trust the guiding Spirit of Infinite Love to lead me, at the right time, into my life's Promised Land.

The success today, in my land of Midian, is attracting unto me the greater influence and power in my Court of Pharaoh, and in my leadership, as I lead others into that promised land which the Lord has prepared for me and mine.

I smile—I sing—I rejoice, and offer thanksgiving and gratitude for my success now and forever. Surely I believe more and more: "My thoughts are not your thoughts, neither are my ways your ways, saith the Lord," and all things are now working together for my good.

Therefore, I have faith and conviction in my ultimate success—in my greater success—in my greatest success!

Abundance

"There is abundance in the world for me given by the bountiful hand of Omnipotence. I gratefully claim and accept all the supply for my needs."

The old idea of orthodox prayer was that of supplication and begging. I have spent a whole night at a time begging for a few pennies and supplicating for the salvation of others. What waste of energy. Each time that we send up such a weak supplication as the attitude of a beggar, with the timid, frightful thoughts that only a beggar's mind can have—this condition of mind, cross circuits the power to bring into our lives the very things we most desire.

When the beggar extends his hand for a copper, he knows that not everyone who passes is going to give him a coin. He, therefore, solicits more or less mechanically, with a mind not positive or sure. His hand is extended in timidity and weakness. Now and then he gets a coin from a sympathetic passer-by. The same principle holds true for the man who prays in the old orthodox fashion. He utters his petitions with doubts and misgivings, with timidity and wonderings. Some of his prayers are answered—just as the occasional coin is cast to the beggar. But most of the orthodox prayers sent up in the fashion of begging and supplicating are never answered. Of necessity, they cannot be, because the concentration is filled with fear and trembling.

Only by positive and courageous thinking do we attract to ourselves the answers to our prayers. When we are permeated with the spirit of doubt, our petitions are cross-circuited.

Therefore, in making your affirmation this time, rest assured that the abundant spirit of the Universal Supply has everything you need, and has it now. You have only to put your mind in a condition to receive.

You do not have to beg the sun for its rays, nor God for His love. It is there for the taking. Many of us keep the sunshine of abundance out of our lives by pulling down the curtain of doubt—just as we may go into a room, pull down a shade and keep out the sun. James Russell Lowell, seventy-five years ago, told us the same story in "The Vision of Sir Launfal," when he said that "Heaven is given away and God may be had for the asking".

By gratefully accepting all of the supply for your needs, you are running up the shade of positive faith and letting the sunlight of abundance in.

Send out the desire for your supply to the Universal Mind and then rest—feeling that it has been acquired. Of course, the stronger you concentrate, without stress and strain (as outlined in "Practical Psychology and Sex Life," by the author, under the chapter "How to get what you want," and chapters on "Concentration"), and the more positive and courageous your concentration, the stronger will be your mental thought currents and consequently the quicker your demonstration.

Omnipotence has provided for me and mine, I raise the shade of my faith and let in the Sunlight of Abundance. I know I do not have to beg for this, for it is mine now. When first I saw the light of day, the bountiful spirit of the Father made all preparations for my life's necessities and pleasures. They have been in the world since I was born. I now claim and accept my supply.

From now on the spirit goes before me—making easy and prosperous all my ways—and I have abundance for every need. From the bountiful hand of Omnipotence I have abundant health—I have abundant love—I have abundant prosperity—I have abundant peace. My Father careth for the grass of the field and the birds of the air—and He careth for me. I realize it.

Think it and live it now.

Abundance for all my needs is mine, now and forever.

Health, Success, Prosperity, Universal Peace and Brotherhood

"God Made From One Blood All the Nations of the World."

As I enter the Silence this time, expecting to get health, success, prosperity and happiness, I am going to have my mind filled with the Spirit of Divine Unity. Unity among the nations of the world, unity in abundance, unity in love, unity in prosperity, unity in health and unity in spirit.

There can be no separation in Spirit. All is Mind, all is God, all is Universal Energy. I am part of the creative force. I am a part and parcel of the Unity of Love, Nature and God. Therefore, where God is, I recognize a completeness. And I, being a part of God, a part of this spirit, a part of the power with Him, am, therefore, at one with God and all thought.

I am therefore at one with God and all spirit. Nothing can separate me from the love of God, but my own mental attitude. Nothing can separate me from abundance, happiness, success, prosperity and love, but my own wrong thinking. Love is dealt in the world in the spirit of God and, therefore, recognizing this unity of love, I am a part of it and have perfect love, success, prosperity, abundance and health.

The ocean is composed of water. If I take a bucket of water from the ocean, it still is the water of the ocean. I may take this water to an island in the sea. Though I have separated this water from the main body of the ocean, it still is the water from the sea. But, as the water is separated from the main body of the ocean, it loses its power, its strength and many of its cardinal properties. I am the same as the sea water when I, by wrong thinking:—whether it be jealousy, envy, hatred, misunderstanding, worry or fear—separate myself from the spirit of God. I am as one going upon an island of humanity. I am still of that same spirit; but it has been separated, so that within me, it has lost many of its cardinal virtues. These virtues are there, but I do not recognize them. Separation has lessened my strength, my vitality, my power, my health, my happiness, my prosperity and my joy.

Just as it is necessary for the bucket of water to remain in the ocean in order to contain all of its original power and to retain all of its original strength, to be intact, so is it necessary for man to keep in the spirit of at-one-ment with the Father, that we may manifest daily God's principle of Unity with God, man and nature.

When we have maintained that attitude of one-ness with the Father in all respects, we are then recognizing and expecting, in this act, the fullness of our spirit. This fullness of our spirit will, therefore, give us health, prosperity and happiness.

When I have a mind that is filled with negative, discordant or inharmonious thoughts, I am separating myself from the full expression of the Divine within me. I am the bucket of water going stale on a human island; but, when I make my spirit at one with the Father by harmonious thinking, by love, kindness, good will, fellowship and co-operation, I am not only maintaining all of my original properties, but I am in correspondence with the Infinite Spirit so that I can manifest and express His original spirit in every particular.

Where there is a unity of spirit, there is unity of all the good things of life. Perhaps I am not drawing from the bank of life's experience everything that I ought to have—because I have separated myself from the spiritual board of directors in this bank of life, and am not getting my dividends on time. My mental attitude is the cause; therefore, as I enter the Silence this time, I am going to maintain the faith and the love-spirit of my unity with all things. I maintain, therefore, my at-one-ment with God, with man and nature. I maintain that all of the original strength of spirit is mine. I hold that the manifestations of this original spirit will produce everything in my life for my ultimate good, because I am at one with the Father. All things are mine.

The Silence, this day, finds me at one with all. The Silence, this day, finds me at peace with God, Man and Nature. The Silence, this day, finds me in at-one-ment with God and all, in unity with every conceivable thing in the universe. Therefore, my unity, my at-one-ment with the Father, my wholeness of spirit with God brings into my life everything for my good.

All things work together for my good in my at-one-ment with Man, God and Nature—in my unity with all.

How to Have More

"I Am Unselfish in Action, Being and Motive."

The science of psychology as applied to everyday life is, strictly speaking, a new science. It is a matter of thousands of people in the world all of a sudden coming in contact with certain laws, which make them successful, healthy and prosperous.

It is quite natural, because man is interested more in himself than in any one else, that, when he finds these laws may be applied to give him more abundance, the tendency may be to use these laws for selfish purposes.

Nothing could be more unpsychological. The laws should be used for the individual, but should not stop there. Each individual who is profiting by the operation of the laws, or understanding of psychology, ought not only to get everything himself that psychology can give him, but he should pass these on to others; he should tell others about it; he should cry it from the housetops and megaphone it from the street corners. He should not want to get everything himself, but wish the same that he has to everyone else. By doing this, the law will rebound, and, instead of having less, he will have still more than he would have were he thinking about the laws for himself alone.

The human race is made up of a whole lot of selfishness, and the man, or the woman, who hopes to get the most out of life and out of psychology, must learn at the very beginning of his or her understanding of the laws. Then, only, will the best come to those who are absolutely unselfish.

If there is any selfish motive or selfish desire in your heart, you may operate the law and get a certain amount of benefit, nay, you may even become rich by it and have great power, but it should not end there. Your riches are for the use of others, as well as for yourselves, and the real psychologist, in getting his riches, will pass on to others that which he has. The real psychologist, in getting more power, will share it with others and will use it for the good of others, as well as for his own personal aggrandizement.

Therefore hold the thought: "I am unselfish in action, being and motive."

Many a person never will get the demonstrations he wants, because the channel of abundance and prosperity, happiness and joy, is clogged up with his own selfish attitude. The selfish person who does operate the laws, does so by overbalancing his selfishness with some other great virtue. But when he is extremely selfish, he may never have demonstrations as he wants; he may not have enough other virtues to outweigh his selfishness. He may live for years, and know what the laws are, and yet lack this one little thing, *unselfishness*, in operating the laws for his own abundance, prosperity or happiness.

If you are not having the demonstrations you want, it is because there is a kink in the mind somewhere. The kink may be selfishness, or it may be pride, haughtiness, duplicity, dishonesty, hatred, envy or jealousy.

This time we are going to hold the thought: "I am unselfish in action, being and motive," and each time we go into the Silence, this unselfish spirit shall be the guiding-star of our thoughts. It will be the personal touch with the Infinite Spirit itself.

The beginning of life's happiness, as well as the end thereof, is the spirit of unselfishness.

BUSH

"I am unselfish in action, being and motive."

All Things are in Divine Order

"Divine Harmony and Peace Actuate Every Thought and Action of My Being."

I realize that all things are in Divine order for me and mine. There can be no disturbance in the world without or the world within my being but that is in perfect harmony with the Infinite.

The circumstances outside of my life are all for my good. My environment where I am now and the conditions in which I am living, I make harmonize for me by my attitude of mind. I think only peace, I breathe only love, I speak only harmony. My conditions and my environment, although outwardly inharmonious to my likes and tendencies, are changed by the alchemy of my thinking into a perfect symphony of happiness for me now.

"Divine Harmony and Peace actuate every thought and action of my being." This thought is energy, this thought is life, this thought is power. The energy, life and power of this thought weaves all of my diversified Life's experiences into a Divine pattern of perfection for me. There can be no trouble, disappointments, sorrow, reverses, loss or discord but that shall be changed for my good when I think Spirit and live the affirmation of today, namely, "Divine Harmony and Peace actuate every thought and action of my being." All things are in Divine order.

The Spirit of Divinity prompts my thinking. The Divine within me actuates my actions. The God Powers within, this minute are working all things together for my good. There can be no danger come nigh my dwelling for my body is the temple of the living God. Therefore, the God Spirit within me protects me from all harm, inspires me to high ideals, lifts me to heights of righteousness and fills my soul with love. Love for my circumstances, love for my present conditions, love for my environment, love for every one in the world, love for all of the creation of God.

Therefore I have no enemies, for I love all. I recognize no misfortunes, for the love energy within turns all misfortunes and sorrows into stepping stones for my greater advancement and achievement. The God energy within transforms all inharmonious conditions without into a perfect harmony within. The Kingdom of God now reigns within me and I am at ease, at peace and at-one-ment with all nature and God. The harmony therefore within me in nature and in God gives me perfect peace within and perfect peace without. Divine thought and energy, love and blessing actuate every action of my being.

Where Divine Love reigns there can be no trouble, no discord, no inharmony, no lack, no limitation, no sorrow, no grief, no sickness, no failure. The energy of Divine Love transforms all things into my Good. The Love and Peace of the Father abideth within me and is manifested without so that my life is one harmonious whole touching the lives of all others who come in contact with me so that they, too, feel my vibrations of at-onement with the Father and they in turn become harmonious and complete in Spirit with man and God.

Divine Harmony and Peace actuate every thought and action of my being. All things are in Divine order.

Thought to Hold in Silence and to Meditate Upon During the Day

FOR JUSTICE

"There's a Spirit of Justice that Secures me in Which is My Own."

If we reach a consciousness of justice, we need have no doubts as to our care in every particular while journeying between the two peaks of eternity—from birth to the Great Divide.

There is nothing that can defeat justice; and the person who has a consciousness of justice will attract to himself every conceivable thing needed for this life, because it will be the logical objective of justice to supply to each individual that justice for which he thinks.

That is the reason why this affirmation is so complete in itself; namely, "There is a spirit of JUSTICE that secures me in which is my own, and this security is provided already for us by the Spirit of Justice."

It would be a psychological paradox to think that Justice could be defeated. That could not be. Perhaps it appears to you that your own has not yet been secured to you, but, remember that life is fleeting—that a year is as a tale that is told—and that a decade is but as "Ships that pass in the night"—when the years have vanished in the distance.

If you have lived a life of justice, and it appears now that your own is not coming to you, that someone else is having more of the good things of life than you, and that someone seems to have used the art of the man of injustice, be not deceived, God is not mocked, for "whatsoever a man soweth that shall he also reap." If you have sowed equity and justice in the days that are gone, be sure that the same equity and justice will be secured to you.

The Scriptures tell us not to think too much of the man who is nourishing like a green bay tree, for his efforts are soon cut off and he vanisheth away.

One who is astride the scales of justice, and who thinks that he can hold the balance, is gravely mistaken. He may have occupied his present position for many years, first putting his weight on one side and then on the other in an effort to keep his equilibrium. Perhaps today it appears that the scales of justice are being well manipulated by his insincerity, duplicity or trickery—but it is like the green bay tree. It will soon pass away.

Justice is as eternal as God Himself, and there is no more possibility of defeating it in the individual's life, in your own life, in the life of a nation or in the history of mankind, than there is likelihood that the sun can get away from its own rays. The justice of God is eternal, or, in other words, God always is Justice, personified. Where God rules, and where His laws and mandates have been given by His own fiat, "man, neither flesh nor the devil" can defeat the ultimate outcome of justice. Your own is secured to you.

Man himself is fashioned by the finger of Divinity. The crown of justice is placed upon his brow and no ruthless hand of greed, duplicity or evil dexterity can ever tear it away. It is there to stay, and the man who has been thus crowned because he has lived in this consciousness of justice—in the consciousness of God Himself—is bound to have come back to him that which he has thought, that which he has sowed—Justice. You are secured by this spirit of justice.

Perhaps already your life has had the law of compensation bring to you more than to others of whom you may think, and who, because of their bank account, get more out of life than you. A man may have a million dollars, and yet not be as happy as the laborer living in a thatched cottage. *Perhaps Justice has tipped the scales in your favor already—and you have failed to recognize it. Perhaps you have children, loved ones, family and fireside which bring more comfort to you than the land owner gets who lives in his palace on the hill.*

Half of Life, or the joys of Life, depend upon our ability to recognize and appreciate the blessings we already have. Therefore, in counting your blessings, or discounting your blessings, be sure that you use a moral standard, instead of a material standard, in gauging whether justice has been meted out to you or not.

The Justice of the Eternal secures me, the Spirit of Justice secures me in which is mine own. Believe it, think it, live it, claim it and Justice shall be yours.

* * * * *

Question—In practicing the Silence, the mind seems to flutter all about and there is great nervous tension. What is wrong?

Answer—Lack of concentration. This person ought to follow some simple exercise of concentration, such as given below, until the mind has control over the body. By practicing a few of the simple exercises given below, fifteen minutes a day, and then taking the Silence a few hours after these exercises have been practiced, the mind will begin to be under control.

The nervous tension is caused because of this lack of control, and in the effort to bring the scattering mind into one focus the reaction comes upon the nervous system which, in turn, reacts upon the body.

Practice and exercises for lack of concentration follow.

EXERCISES

By Thos. Parker Boyd

(1) Select some part of the body, a foot or hand, with the idea of HEAT. While holding the mind in this attitude, breathe deeply and steadily, and, in from one to four minutes, you will feel the warm glow coming to the foot. In this way, you can soon master the entire body. Begin with the sense of feeling. If there is an itching of the body, make it stop by the force of your will. In from three days to three weeks, you can stop the itching sensation at will. Then try the habit of sneezing; stubbornly resist the inclination to sneeze, and you will soon have the mastery. Now try your will on coughing. When the tickling sensation comes, stop it by the exercise of your will. You can soon master it. Next try it on pain. When you feel a pain in the body, instead of rubbing on liniment, rub in a little will power; soon it will ease your pain as if by magic. With the fingers of one hand rub the skin on the back of the other hand, stroking toward the elbow, and will that all feeling shall disappear. In from one to three minutes, take a needle, and you can stick it through the skin on the back of the hand without pain. You may have to try it a dozen times, but persistence will bring success. Having mastered the sense of feeling, take up that of hearing.

(2) It may seem impossible at first thought, but you have seen people so absorbed in what they were reading or thinking that they heard nothing, although you addressed them directly. They are simply abstracted from all else, and are thinking of one thing—to the exclusion of everything else. They entered this state of abstractedness unconsciously. To do so intentionally, you go by the law of indirectness. For instance, take sight; concentrate your vision and your whole attention upon some object, real or imaginary, until soon the sense of HEARING becomes dormant. A little practice will enable you to study, think or sleep, regardless of noise.

(3) Having mastered hearing, begin on SIGHT. You have known people who walked on the street, looked at you and passed by without recognition, although they knew you well. A person deeply thinking on some subject, neither sees nor hears, but uses the mental sense entirely. The method is to let the eyes be open, but concentrate the thoughts on hearing or feeling.

(4) After getting control of your sight, take up the TASTE. Take some tasteless thing on the tongue, abstract the mind to something else until the taste becomes dormant. Then take something with more taste to it, abstracting the taste, until by this gradual process you can make the sourest pickle sweet.

(5) Finally take some light odor, and hold it before the nostrils, abstracting the attention from the sense of smell, by hearing or seeing, etc., until by practice you can pass through the foulest odor without inconvenience or notice.

Sit or stand absolutely motionless, except your breathing, for one to five minutes at a time. Do this often.

Practice closing each finger in rotation; then, when all are closed, open one at a time very slowly, keeping the attention fixed on what you are doing. Keep all the other fingers still, save the one you are exercising with.

Inhale gradually for ten seconds, then exhale in the same way and time.

Look steadily at some point or object for a minute without winking the eye, keeping your attention fixed on the object.

Look at a picture critically, then close your eyes and mentally reconstruct it.

Close your eyes and construct the face of a friend, feature by feature.

Fix your attention on a hand or foot, hold on it the idea of heat and continue until the hand or foot feels warm. Then try cold; then try pain.

Will that the person in front of you shall turn around or put his hand on his head or neck.

Hold your hand on some one in pain and say, "I will the pain to depart." Repeat till the pain goes.

Note.—For a scientific understanding of positive and negative concentration, see "Practical Psychology and Sex Life," by the author.

Silent Treatment

Those at a distance or those who cannot attend my classes may have silent treatments—distance is no barrier—race or creed no bar to those who earnestly want to benefit from the Silent Treatment.

Many marvelous cures have been reported through Silent Treatment. Business has been increased, positions secured, bad habits broken, prosperity demonstrated, peace and harmony restored in home and business.

This is one of the strongest of Dr. Bush's study features. Use blank on opposite page for yourself, your friends or those whom you desire to help. You may begin it at any time.

You will get the vibration of the campaign and the power of thousands of minds working for you and with you for your health and happiness.

These silent treatments will help the sick rise above disease, overcome despair, and bring to themselves the positive healing vibration of Dr. Bush and his class.

USE BLANK ON NEXT PAGE AND BOLD THE THOUGHT OF THE DEMONSTRATION YOU DESIRE—THERE IS NO FEE. GIVE IN PROPORTION AS YOU HOPE TO SECURE. "FREELY

YE HAVE RECEIVED, FREELY GIVE." THE LAW OF COMPENSATION DEMONSTRATES THIS TRUTH.

Notes

[1: Taken from Applied Psychology and Scientific Living.]

[2: For complete study of how to charge the subconscious mind, see chapters on the "Subconscious Mind," "How to Cleanse the Aura," "How to Get What You Want," "Concentration" and "Visualization," in "Practical Psychology and Sex Life" by the author.]

[3: Scientific explanation of the Silence and How to enter the Silence and the benefits derived thereby, will be found in "Practical Psychology and Sex Life" by David V. Bush.]

[4: This is from The Fundamentals of Applied Psychology.]

[5: This is from Applied Psychology and Scientific Living.]

Also from Benediction Books ...

Wandering Between Two Worlds: Essays on Faith and Art
Anita Mathias
Benediction Books, 2007
152 pages
ISBN: 0955373700

Available from www.amazon.com, www.amazon.co.uk

In these wide-ranging lyrical essays, Anita Mathias writes, in lush, lovely prose, of her naughty Catholic childhood in Jamshedpur, India; her large, eccentric family in Mangalore, a sea-coast town converted by the Portuguese in the sixteenth century; her rebellion and atheism as a teenager in her Himalayan boarding school, run by German missionary nuns, St. Mary's Convent, Nainital; and her abrupt religious conversion after which she entered Mother Teresa's convent in Calcutta as a novice. Later rich, elegant essays explore the dualities of her life as a writer, mother, and Christian in the United States--Domesticity and Art, Writing and Prayer, and the experience of being "an alien and stranger" as an immigrant in America, sensing the need for roots.

About the Author

Anita Mathias was born in India, has a B.A. and M.A. in English from Somerville College, Oxford University and an M.A. in Creative Writing from the Ohio State University. Her essays have been published in The Washington Post, The London Magazine, The Virginia Quarterly Review, Commonweal, Notre Dame Magazine, America, The Christian Century, Religion Online, The Southwest Review, Contemporary Literary Criticism, New Letters, The Journal, and two of HarperSanFrancisco's The Best Spiritual Writing anthologies. Her non-fiction has won fellowships from The National Endowment for the Arts; The Minnesota State Arts Board; The Jerome Foundation, The Vermont Studio Center; The Virginia Centre for the Creative Arts, and the First Prize for the Best General Interest Article from the Catholic Press Association of the United States and Canada. Anita has taught Creative Writing at the College of William and Mary, and now lives and writes in Oxford, England.

www.anitamathias.com,
christiancogitations.blogspot.com
wanderingbetweentwoworlds.blogspot.com

www.ingramcontent.com/pod-product-compliance
Lightning Source LLC
LaVergne TN
LVHW050947080826
845145LV00004B/1437